Contents

Written by Catherine Baker

Illustrated by Diego Vaisberg

Collins

Put the rubbish out

3

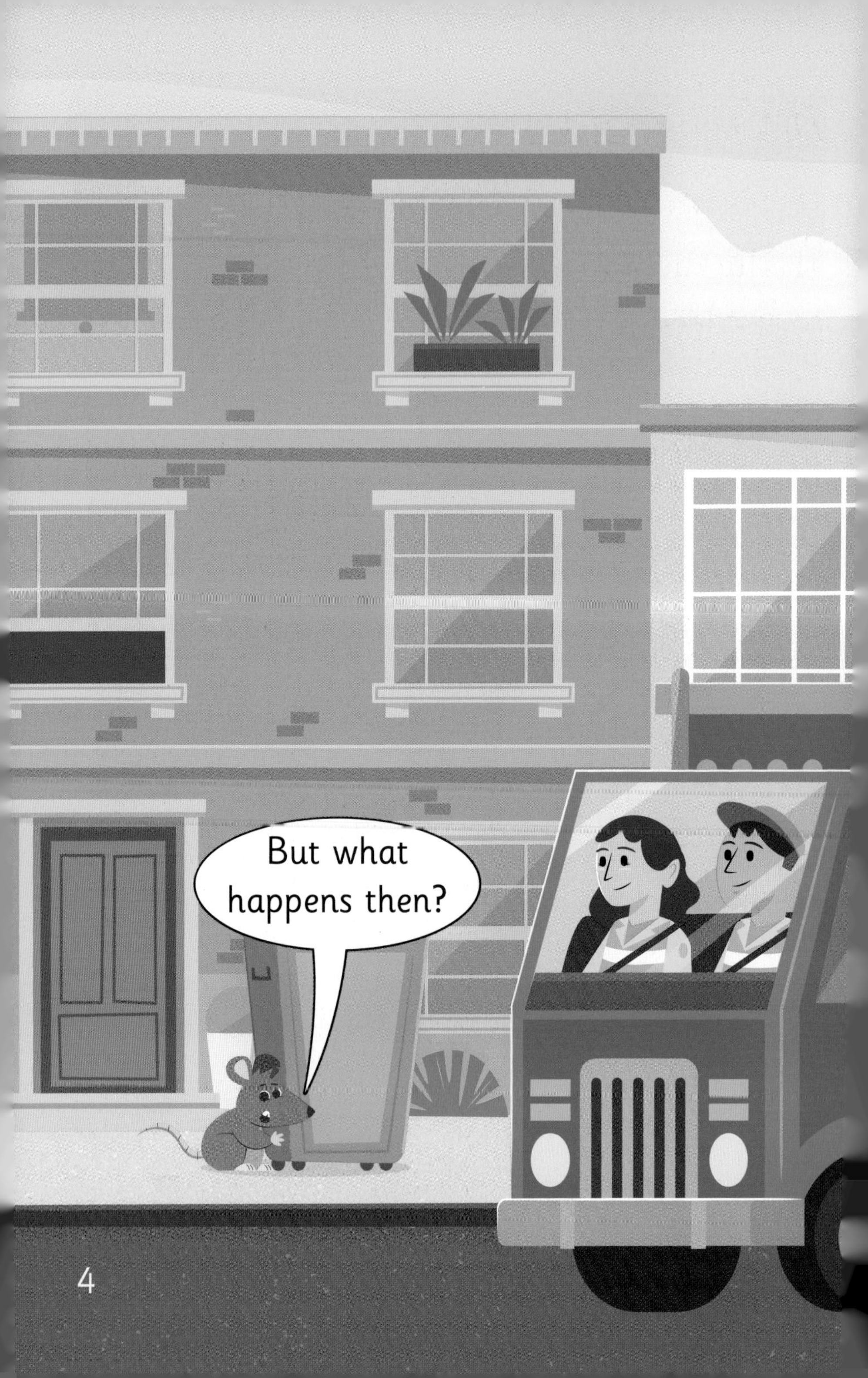
But what happens then?

The rubbish truck

This is what happens to the rubbish next!

1. The rubbish truck comes to pick up
   the bins.

2. The bin lifts up, and the rubbish thumps into the truck.

7

3. Then the truck chugs off with all
the rubbish.

9

Rubbish check

4. In the shed, the rubbish gets a full check.

Metal rubbish

5. Then a magnet will lift up some of
the metal cans.

Plastic rubbish

6. All the plastics get a scan to check what they are. Then the different plastics are split up.

15

Melted rubbish

7. When the different plastics and metals are split up, they get melted.

Fresh objects

8. When the metal and plastic is melted, fresh objects can be constructed.

Glossary

fish out pull out

magnetic Magnetic objects can be lifted by a magnet.

shredded When you shred objects, you chop them into bits.

stash put

Index

What happens to rubbish?

After reading

Letters and Sounds: Phases 3 and 4

Word count: 214

Focus phonemes: /ch/ /sh/ /th/, and adjacent consonants

Common exception words: of, to, the, I, into, all, by, put, pull, full, push, are, we, be, you, they, like, so, some, comes, when, out, what

Curriculum links: Science: Forces and magnets; States of matter

National Curriculum learning objectives: Reading/word reading: apply phonic knowledge and skills as the route to decode words; read accurately by blending sounds in unfamiliar words containing GPCs that have been taught; read common exception words, noting unusual correspondences between spelling and sound and where these occur in words; read other words of more than one syllable that contain taught GPCs; Reading/comprehension (KS2): understand what they read, in books they can read independently, by checking that the text makes sense to them, discussing their understanding and explaining the meaning of words in context

Developing fluency

- Read the book together with your child, encouraging your child to use a different voice for the rat's speech bubbles.
- Check that your child uses an upward tone for questions and a surprised tone for sentences ending in exclamation marks.

Phonic practice

- Practise reading words with adjacent consonants:
  crisps   stash   end   next   shred
- Challenge your child to read the following words with more than one syllable. If necessary, encourage them to sound out and blend each syllable.
  page 2: rubbish (*rubb ish*)   page 3: collected (*coll ect ed*)
  page 18: constructed (*con-struct-ed*)

Extending vocabulary

- Look together at the glossary on page 20. Decide on glossary definitions for the following words. Ask your child to check their meanings in context.
  page 3: push (e.g. *roll*)   page 8: chugs (e.g. *moves slowly making a noise*
  page 18: fresh (e.g. *clean, new*)   *like a train*)